FICTION HOUSE PRESS
PRESENTS

HELLO BUDDIES

November-December 1959
Issue No. 96

This reprint edition is a facsimile of the original pulp magazine. Variations in printing and quality can be attributed to the original magazine which was printed on rough woodpulp paper. No attempt has been made to politically correct any language deemed inappropriate to the modern reader.

ISBN 978-1-64720-581-2

www.FictionHousePress.com
fictionhousepress@gmail.com

Cecil! Don't you dare wish that!

NOV. - DEC., 1959—Issue No. 96
Leon Harvey, Editor

HELLO Buddies

It's not that I don't love you Herbert—it's merely that you bore the daylights out of me!

JUDY: He's very handsome.

TRUDY: Yes, but he has a set of false teeth.

JUDY: How do you know?

TRUDY: It came out in the course of conversation!

* * *

CUTIE: I'd like a cigar for my husband.

SALESMAN: Strong or mild?

CUTIE: Strong, so the ashes won't keep breaking off it!

* * *

LAURA: I can't make up my mind which man to marry.

FLORA: It doesn't make any difference.

LAURA: What do you mean it doesn't make any difference?

FLORA: Which ever one you marry you'll be sorry you didn't marry the other one!

HELLO BUDDIES published bi-monthly by FUN PARADE, at 420 DeSoto Avenue, St Louis 7, Mo. Editorial, executive and advertising offices at 1860 Broadway, New York 23, N. Y. Entered as second class matter at the Post Office in St. Louis, Mo. Single copy 25 cents. Subscription rate in U. S. and possessions only, five issues for $1.00. Publisher accepts no responsibility for loss of unsolicited material. Permission granted for reproduction in service and school periodicals only. All names in this periodical are entirely fictitous and no identification with actual persons is intended.
65
Printed in U.S.A.

Look insulted—but not too insulted!

Don't worry, Mrs. Smith—if your husband is running around with other women, I'll get the goods on the low down rat!

Pull up a chair, honey. I'm a chain smoker!

PIN-UP PARADE

DOLORES OF THE CHORUS: I'd like another checkbook for that aaccount you opened for me.

SUGAR DADDY: What happened to the checkbook you had a few days ago?

DOLORES OF THE CHORUS: I lost it. But don't look so worried—I signed all the checks as soon as I got it, so it won't be any use to anyone who finds it!

* * *

GUY: Why do girls sometimes carry money in their bosoms?

GAL: Because they want to bank their wealth where it'll draw the most interest!

* * *

ACTRESS: I used to curse the day I was born. Did you ever do that?

ACTOR: No, I didn't learn to curse until I was about five years old!

This is even better than I figured!

I'm winded, honey. Don't know what we'd do without our young, husky neighbor!

WOMAN: I'm sixty-two years old and have never been kissed. Did I miss anything?

MAN: It's too late to find out now!

* * *

"Do you sometimes have doubts about your boy-friend's love being genuine?"

"Yes, I don't think he really loves half the other girls he says he loves!"

* * *

"Can I kiss you?"

"How am I supposed to know?"

* * *

MARY: Imagine! Some fresh guy offered me a dollar for a kiss.

ANN: What are you searching for?

MARY: I think I lost the dollar!

Wow! Did we just have a coffee break!

Is this the Smith Holding Company?
It sure is!

You overslept? You mean you sleep at home, too?

JONES: Be like me—an optimist.

BONES: How's that?

JONES: I don't care what happens—as long .as it happens to someone else!

* * *

JIM: Boy, I though that was the funniest thing when that guy fed you a laxative and you thought it was chocolate.

TIM: Yeah, I had to hold my stomach!

* * *

WILL: Who's the boss in your house?

BILL: Well, Sally is in charge of the children, the house, the maid and the dog. But I can do pretty much what I darn please with the goldfish!

* * *

MOVIE ACTRESS: I'm divorcing you, James. I need a Latin type for the new house!

Think it will spread next door?

That new maid of ours does everything!

domess-tickles

HUBBY: I just got a letter from the bank saying that you've overdrawn your checking account!

WIFEY: Oh, I've already attended to that, dear. I sent the bank a check to cover the amount I overdrew!

* * *

MRS. BROWN: How are you?

MRS. GREEN: Wonderful! My husband had a stroke and we're going to Florida for the winter!

* * *

SON: I heard that married men live longer than single men.

FATHER: That's not true—it only seems longer!

* * *

"Why do you call your wife, "Sweets?"

"Because sweets have always disagreed with me!"

Well, there go my Sundays!

But I'm not sleepy yet, Vivian!

She's drinking champagne. Still want to meet her?

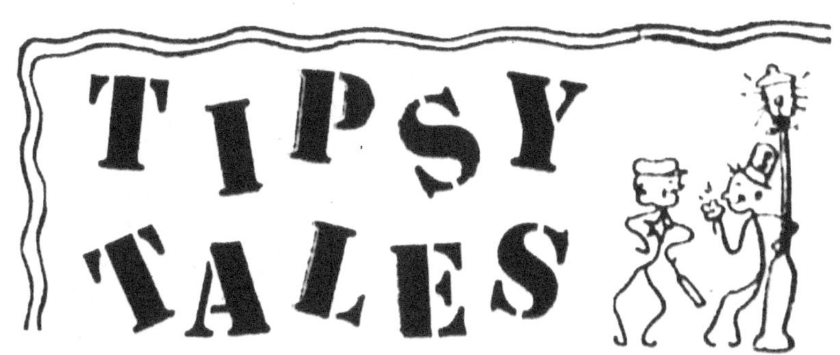

SOUSE: What time is it?

SOT: It's not midnight yet.

SOUSE: How do you know?

SOT: Because I told my wife I'd be home by midnight—and I'm not there yet!

* * *

"My father fell down a flight of stairs with a quart of whiskey."

"Did he spill the whiskey?"

"No, he kept his mouth shut!"

* * *

1ST DRUNK: What's your name?

2ND DRUNK: John

1ST DRUNK: I mean, what's your full name?

2ND DRUNK: It's John—empty or full!

* * *

"Let's go downtown to a bar."

"Can't. I'm minding the baby."

"What? Are you and Helen married?"

"No, but she made me give up drinking, and I'm minding her!"

It's just like Bingo—only faster!

I must say you certainly have a different approach, Edgar!

Nice try, Miss Goldbrick, but that's the same excuse you used to get off early last week!

That gives me a headache!

Don't worry about my husband, Mr. Jordan. He's always wanted me to have these things!

Been doing a little window shopping on my lunch hour!

MAN: Could I see the man who was arrested for breaking into my house last night?

WARDEN: Why do you want to see him?

MAN: I want to ask him how he managed to get in without waking up my wife!

* * *

LAWYER: Do you believe your sweetheart's death was the result of a broken heart?

CUTIE: Of course. If he hadn't broken my heart I wouldn't have shot him!

* * *

JUDGE: Why do you want a divorce?

WOMAN: Because every time I sit on my husband's lap he starts to dictate letters!

* * *

CUTIE: Officer, I want to charge my boyfriend with reckless driving.

POLICEMAN: What's reckless about his driving?

CUTIE: He was driving with another girl!

It was like this, honey. We were parked on Shady Road, darling, and all of a sudden, without provocation, he—play close attention, baby—he . . .

No. Long Beach is a little more to the east. That would be Asbury Park over there!

Wait until they eat as much as I do!

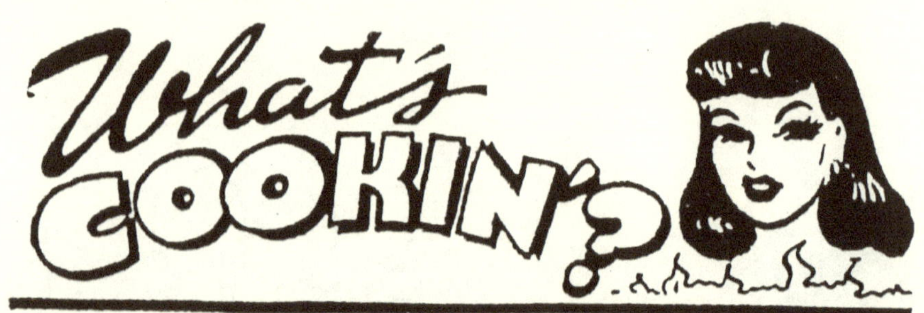

MRS. JONES: My husband and I passed a hat shop soon after we were married, and I saaw the cutest little hat. So that night I cooked my husband a really grand dinner. Then I snuggled up close to him and said, "What will I get if I keep baking pies like that everyday for you"?

MRS. BONES: And what did he say?

MRS. JONES: "My life insurance!"

* * *

WIFE: How did you like that chocolate custard dessert I made?

HUSBAND: It was awful.

WIFE: That's funny the cookbook said it was delicious!

* * *

GIRLFRIEND: The two best things I make are chocolate cake and liver dumplings.

BOYFRIEND: Well, which is this?

You'll be wise to tip him ten dollars—
he's my husband!

I think we'd better thin it out with water!

Something FOR THE BOYS

JACK: I got into a show free last night.

MACK: How come?

JACK: The other guy paid!

* * *

GUY: Why do you always wear such funny-looking clothes?

GAL: Well, once I didn't wear them, and they threw me into jail!

* * *

LOOIE: Are you going to Mary's big party tomorrow night?

BLOOIE: No, I have some business to attend to out of town.

LOOIE: I didn't get invited either!

* * *

RUDY: I found out what kind of costume you're supposed to wear to the party, and you're not gonna like it.

TRUDY: Why, what is it?

RUDY: You're supposed to dress to match your date's hair—and I'm bald!

Don't let him talk you into fastening the safety belt!

Of course I love you, stupid!

You're now on time and a half, Miss Bates. Would you like to try for double time?

from nine 'til five

MRS. JONES: I was terribly sorry to hear that your husband went bankrupt.

MRS. BONES: Oh, yes, and it upset him so much that he's going to retire from business and go abroad!

* * *

"I'm going to start on my second million dollars."

"Your second? You haven't even made one million dollars."

"I know, but I heard that the first million is the hardest—so I'm starting with the second!"

* * *

1ST BUSINESSMAN: There's no business that makes money these days without advertising.

2ND BUSINESSMAN: I know a business that makes money without advertising.

1ST BUSINESSMAN: What's that?

2ND BUSINESSMAN: The mint!

I've been so busy I haven't had a chance to introduce you to each other—Suzie Walker meet Charlie Fignewton!

I get out Saturday—be sure to line up some of the boys for an evening of poker!

FARMER'S WIFE: It's my birthday today. Shall I go out in the yard and kill a chicken to celebrate?

FARMER: Why punish a poor chicken for something that happened many years ago?

* * *

"You know, I have royal blood in my veins. My father was offered a crown twice, but he refused it."

"What was he holding out for, a gold inlay?

* * *

FARMER BROWN: I hear your son's studying farming in college.

FARMER GREEN: No, not farming. He's studying botany.

FARMER BROWN: Botany?

FARMER GREEN: You know . . . flower and plants. He wants to be a naturalist. You know what a naturalist is, don't you?

FARMER BROWN: Sure, a fellow who runs around without clothes on!

But what are birds and bees and flowers?

HANG ON
TO YOUR
HAT

Of course I wouldn't make a play for the boss,
I find personnel managers more desirable!

HER BOYFRIEND: I suppose you're aware that I've been making advances to your daughter.

HER FATHER: Yes, shake, son. And now what about her poor old man?

* * *

MARRIED WOMAN: Married life isn't so very different from being single.

SINGLE GIRL: How is that?

MARRIED WOMAN: You wait up half the night for your boyfriend to go home, and I wait up half the night for my husband to come home.

* * *

GUY: Do you ever take long walks before breakfast?

GAL: That depends upon whose car I've been out in!

* * *

JUDY: Oh, I had a wonderful time last night. He said things to me that no man ever said.

TRUDY: What was that?

JUDY: He asked me to marry him!

Are you following me?

I can take them or leave them alone—it depends on how much they're worth!

DITCH DIGGER: I've been on the job for two whole days and nobody has given me a shovel.

FOREMAN: What are you complaining about? Without a shovel you don't have to do any work.

DITCH DIGGER: Yeah, but I don't have anything to lean on like the other guys do!

* * *

"I'm a self-made man."

"That's what comes of hiring cheap labor!"

* * *

LARRY: How late do you sleep on Sunday mornings?

BARRY: That all depends.

LARRY: What does it depend upon?

BARRY: The length of the sermon!

* * *

"Boy, wasn't that dream I had last night a lulu!"

"How should I know?"

"You were in it!"

I've looked forward to something like this all my life—to fish all day long—and no rod and reel!

We've been here three hours and not a single one has shown up!

Oh, Mr. Lundquist! You hit the nail on the head!

"I'll bet you're one of those guys who drops his work and dashes home the minute it's five o'clock."

"No as a matter of fact, after I quit work I have to wait around quite a while till five o'clock."

* * *

JACK: Well, how have you been?

MACK: I've managed to keep my neck above water.

JACK: I can see that, by the color of it!

* * *

HOTEL MANAGER: Hey! You can't go parading around the lobby in pajamas!

GUEST: Oh, I'm terribly sorry—but you see, I'm a somnambulist.

HOTER MANAGER: I don't care what your religion is—you can't parade around here in pajamas!

ACE

Sure I still love you, but the fact remains there's still a lot of dictation for you to take!

POETIC PARODIES

'ATHLETES'

There are many kinds of 'athletes'
These days—if you want to call them that,
They participate in sports, that is,
—some to keep from getting fat.

Others take up the sport of golf.
Not because it's what they like,
But because it gets them in good with the boss
Who, it just so happens, likes Ike.

Then some guys go in for bowling.
Think they like it? Not on your life!
Either they fear being office wet blanket
Or they want a night off from the wife.

And the guys so devoted to tennis,
Do they like it? Definitely nyet!
It's just that gals are so impressed
When they win and leap over the net.

And the guys who go in for swimming
Do it because they look good in shorts.
Whatever you say about athletes,
One sure thing—they're not sports.

You never notice what I don't wear anymore!

Don't you think you're carrying this "do-it-yourself" stuff a little too far?

Yoo-hoo, doctor! I found your stethoscope!

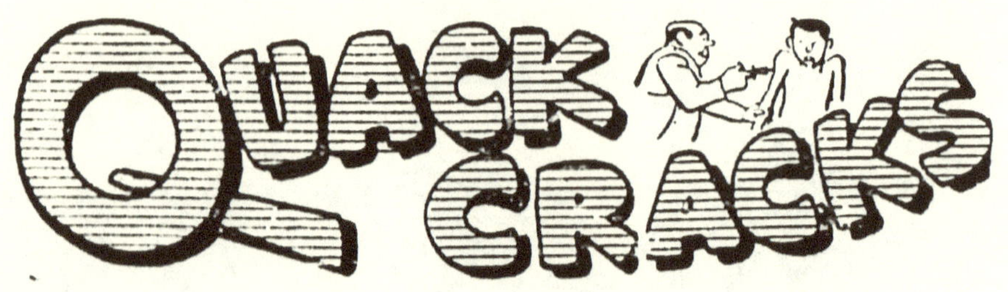

DR. QUACK: I'll have to put down that your husband died of unknown causes.

MRS. MACK: Yes, I still don't know exactly why I poisoned him!

* * *

"I've got another mouth to feed."

"You mean you're . . ."

"I've got a tapeworm!"

* * *

"I've got French blood in me."

"By your father?"

"No, by transfusion!"

* * *

DR. MACK: What's the matter, old boy? You look terrible.

DR. QUACK: I just sent that rich old Mr. Knockafeller the wrong medicine.

DR. MACK: Is it serious?

DR. QUACK: It sure it! The medicine I sent him will cure him in three days!

You didn't have enough affection when you were a little girl—we'll just have to make up for lost time!

Go through all our pants pockets, look under the cushions on the sofa, put your tie on, and rush down here!

RADIO  ROUNDUP

MICHAEL O'SHEA (Satirizing film credits): Nelson Eddy can currently be seen—in the living room of his home in San Fernando Valley.

* * *

IRATE AUTOIST: What's the matter with you—are you blind?
OTHER DRIVER: No sir, I hit you, didn't I?

* * *

BOB HOPE: You say an Eskimo boy can easily tell when his girl has been unfaithful to him?
KINGFISH: Sure, he finds callouses on her nose!

* * *

ARNOLD: Friend of mine brought his bride home and she couldn't make up her mind whether to refer to his mother as mother or mother-in-law.
DOTTIE DILLARD: Well, how'd she solve the problem?
ARNOLD: She just waited a while and then called her gran'ma!

* * *

CORLISS: Well, it seems there was a fat lady who went to a drugstore to weigh herself. But she didn't know the scale was broken and when she stepped on it, it only registered a hundred pounds. A kid watching her yelled, "Hey, look, she's hollow!

Take a letter, Miss Hobson . . . really!

Here I am, Otis! Out here!

Good Lord! I forgot to break my engagement with Joe Vosmik!

JONES: It's no disgrace to work.

BONES: That's what I keep telling my wife!

* * *

MRS.: You never take any good advice.

MR.: No, if I did you'd be an old maid!

* * *

One way for a guy to save money is to marry his second wife first!

* * *

SMITH: Did you ever win an argument with your wife?

JACKSON: Yep, once. Only once.

SMITH: When was that?

JACKSON: I can't remember when it was. All I remember about it was that her mouth was full of hairpins at the time!

It's not that I love you, Eddy—you just remind me of Joe, and I can't resist him!

Your four-leaf clover has brought me luck already, Gerald. Ronny is calling me for a date!

Jimmy and I are through—we gave each other two weeks notice last night!

All right, men. Why is it that Miss Gay always leads in sales?

Let's change the subject and talk about some of my other good points!

That was fun! I can't wait till next time!

SALESMAN: I'd like to see the head of the house.

JUNIOR: Then wait of couple of minutes—they're just deciding it!

*　　　*　　　*

BOBBY: Does m-i-r-a-g-e spell marriage?

FATHER: Yes, son!

*　　　*　　　*

JIMMY: When the light goes out, where does it go?

MOTHER: How should I know? You might just as well ask me where your father goes when he goes out!

*　　　*　　　*

"Is June your oldest sister?"

"Yes."

"And who comes after her?"

"You and a couple of other guys!"

Stay for the geography lesson. I'll tell about some fascinating places to run away to!

What a day!

It's nothing serious!

LANA: I read where a woman just cremated her fourth husband.

ANNA: Isn't that life! Some of us can't get one husband and others have husbands to burn!

* * *

MRS. SMITH: I finally paid off the plumber.

MR. SMITH: Good. Now I can take a shower with a clean conscience!

* * *

CLEM: It's a good idea to buy clothes on the installment plan.

LEM: Why?

CLEM: Because then they give you stuff that will last until the installments are paid!

* * *

WIFE: Spread newspapers in front of the fireplace, dear.

HUSBAND: Why?

WIFE: So if sparks come out they won't get on the rug!

I want you to meet the best darn lawyer that ever went to bat for a guy!

Why can't you be satisfied with a Hip Flask
like other men?

JOE: I dived off the pier and fell into water up to my knees. I would have drowned if a fellow hadn't pulled me out.

BLOW: Don't be silly—you couldn't have drowned in water up to your knees.

JOE: Oh, no? It so happens I went in head first!

* * *

GUY: What well-developed arms you have.

GAL: I play a lot of ping pong and tennis.

GUY: You ride horseback, too, don't you?

* * *

"Poor Jones got so fat he had to give up playing golf."

"Why so?"

"Well, if he put the ball where he could see it then he couldn't hit it, and if he put it where he could hit it he couldn't see it!"

So he told me two could live as cheaply as one, and I told him I didn't want to live cheaply!

I'm sure I'll get the secretarial job—he is my uncle and blood is thicker th—

No openings now, Miss Gay—but I can get you a spot in a penthouse apartment with all the diamonds you can use!

TAKE YOUR OWN
PHOTO 25¢

You've been here three times today—just what are you surveying?

But just because I'm married doesn't mean
I can't be lonely!

CHOCK FULL OF GAGS, GALS, GAIETY!

WHEN YOU PICK IT UP, YOU'LL NEVER PUT IT DOWN!

G. I. FUN 'N' FROLIC!

FAST 'N' FRISKY!

If You Like BUDDIES, You'll Like FUN PARADE!

GET YOUR COPY! NOW ON SALE!

Oh! I wasn't expecting you—my hair must be a sight!

LES: I'd never buy a car. It's much too complicated.

WES: What do you mean?

LES: All I know is my brother is still paying off the car he sold in part payment of the car he has now!

* * *

"One more payment and the car is ours."

"Good! Then we can get rid of it and get a new one!"

* * *

WOMAN: Is this the fire house?

FIREMAN: Yes.

WOMAN: Well, I've just planted a tulip garden and . . .

FIREMAN: Where's the fire?

WOMAN: It took a lot of time and expense to plant . . .

FIREMAN: Look . . . there's a florist down the block.

WOMAN: I don't want a florist. I was coming to the fire in a minute. My neighbor's house is burning and I don't want all you firemen to trample my garden when you go there!

You must be Betty's blind date—I'm
Betty's mother!

I just can't understand why they call you a cheap politician!

PRIVATE
BEACH
KEEP OFF

CAPTAIN FUTURE
WIZARD OF SCIENCE
COMET
FICTION AND FACT OF THE PRIZE-RING
FIGHT STORIES
THE BLACK UHLAN
HEADQUARTERS DETECTIVE
MURDER TREADMILL
G-MAN JUGGERNAUT
MASKED RIDER WESTERN
BORROWED HOSSES
FIGHTING ACES OF WAR SKIES
WINGS
10 STORY WESTERN MAGAZINE
ADVENTURE NOVELS
Thrilling Stories of the Sky Trails
AIR STORIES
THE NIGHT HAWK
GEORGE BRUCE
FIGHTING DAREDEVILS OF TODAY'S WAR
AIR WAR
THE ALL-STORY
WARLORD of MARS
ARMY Romances
BASKETBALL STORIES
Battle Stories
O'LEARY IN ACTION IN ETHIOPIA
All Star Issue of Favorite War Authors
BLACK BOOK DETECTIVE
GOLDEN FLEECE
ROMAN HOLIDAY by TALBOT MUNDY
HIGH-SEAS ADVENTURES
THE SEA ROGUE
CAPTAIN HARDY
ADVENTURES OF THE FIRST AMERICANS
INDIAN Stories
BRIDE of the TOMAHAWK PACK
MY LIFE WITH SITTING BULL
LONE RANGER
MAGIC CARPET MAGAZINE
PEARLS FROM MACAO
H. BEDFORD JONES
MARVEL SCIENCE STORIES
NEW DETECTIVE
DEATH LIVES HERE!
NO BODY BUT YOU
North-West ROMANCES
SATAN'S TIMBER CLAIM
GIRLS of WHITE WATER TRAIL
DAN CUSHMAN
Oriental STORIES
PHANTOM DETECTIVE
THE Deadly DIAMONDS
PLANET stories
QUEEN OF THE MARTIAN CATACOMBS
POPULAR DETECTIVE
DEATH IN A COTTAGE
MURDER INSURANCE
PRIVATE DETECTIVE
LOVE STORIES OF THE REAL WEST
RANCH ROMANCES
Maid of the Valley
RANGE RIDERS
SIX-GUN VALLEY
Vice Squad DETECTIVE
SECRET of the HOUSE of HORROR
TOP-NOTCH STORIES TOP-NOTCH WRITERS
UNDERWORLD DETECTIVE
FIVE FATAL MINUTES
KILLER'S BAIT
THRILLING WONDER STORIES
TIDAL MOON
THE FEDERALS IN ACTION
G-MEN
GIVE 'EM HELL
SCIENCE FICTION
SPICY-ADVENTURE STORIES
HELL'S RIVER

www.ingramcontent.com/pod-product-compliance
Lightning Source LLC
LaVergne TN
LVHW050936080826
845145LV00004B/1280

* 9 7 8 1 6 4 7 2 0 5 8 1 2 *